STAR SIGNS

WRITTEN AND ILLUSTRATED BY

LEONARD EVERETT FISHER

HOLIDAY HOUSE/NEW YORK

ASTRO is a Greek word meaning "star."

LOGOS is a Greek word meaning "talk."

ASTROLOGOS in Greek means "talk about stars."

ASTROLOGY is the study of talking about stars, or more clearly, the study of how things on Earth are tied to the stars in the sky.

NOMOS is a Greek word meaning "law."

ASTRONOMOS in Greek means "law of stars."

ASTRONOMY is the study of the law of stars, or more clearly, the study of laws that govern the movements of all the stars.

Library of Congress Cataloging in Publication Data

Fisher, Leonard Everett.
Star signs.

Summary: Introduces the myths, character traits, symbols, and constellations associated with each sign of the zodiac and explains the origins of astrology and how it differs from astronomy.
1. Zodiac—Juvenile literature. 2. Astrology—Juvenile literature. [1. Zodiac. 2. Astrology. 3. Constellations. 4. Stars] I. Title.
BF1726.F57 1983   133.5′2   83-305
ISBN 0-8234-0491-9

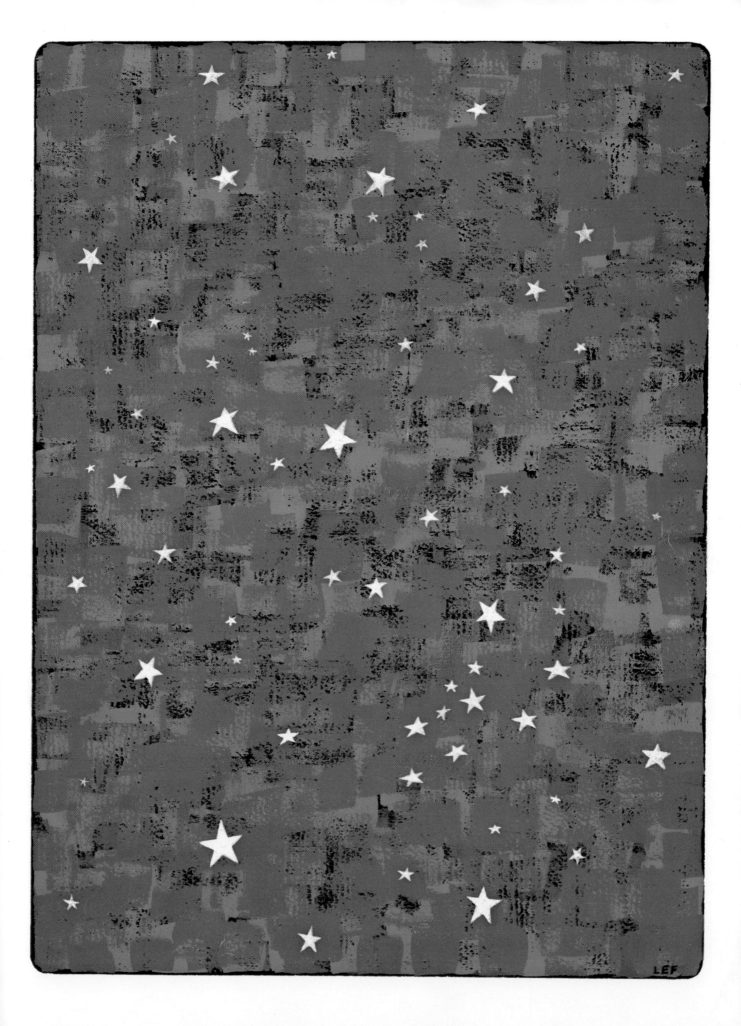

Long before the ancient Greeks made up words for studying the stars and planets, there were other people who studied the heavens.

Sumerian farmers, who lived in what is now southern Iraq, watched the changing skies more than 4,000 years ago. They looked for signs to tell them how to deal with everyday problems and what to expect: when to plant crops, whether the harvest would be good or bad, when to go to war, whether battles would be won or lost. They believed that everything that happened on earth—floods, earthquakes, happiness, success, life, death—was planned in the heavens above.

Whenever Sumerians peered up at the sky, nothing seemed to stand still. Only the Earth seemed to stay in one place. It looked like the sun moved around the Earth about once every 365 days. And the moon rose, then fell each night. It changed shape too—from quarter, to half, to three-quarter, to full moon. Sometimes a scary shadow crept across its bright face. More frightening was the shadow that blocked out the sun once and in a while, turning day into night. From time to time comets with long tails swept across the sky. And meteors sparked the starry night with showers of light. No one knew how these things happened or why. They worshiped the sun and the moon as gods. They did not expect gods to explain themselves to people. The Sumerians kept records of the movement of the sun, moon, and stars. Also, they kept records of what went on in their lives every day. They looked for patterns in the sky that could explain what happened on Earth.

Soon there were other "gods" in the heavens. About 2,600 years ago, the Chaldean Babylonians discovered five planets they thought were gods. Today, we call these planets Mercury, Venus, Mars, Saturn, and Jupiter, names first used by the Romans. The Chaldeans thought these planets caused everything that happened on Earth. And it was the job of Chaldean priests to keep track of the planet-gods, to watch their movements, and to decide what they meant.

The priests decided that the Earth stood still at the center of the universe. They thought an invisible band ran around the Earth through which the sun, the moon, and the five planets traveled. This band was called the zodiac. The zodiac was divided into twelve equal parts or houses.

The Egyptians and others borrowed most of these ideas from the Chaldeans. A Greek named Herodotus wrote them down about 2,400 years ago. The Greeks renamed each house in the zodiac after a constellation or fixed group of stars. Constellations like Aquarius or Gemini became signs of the zodiac. Each house now stood for a part of the calendar year. The Greeks made charts based on the zodiac. They thought these charts would help them tell the future for any moment of time—day, hour, or minute. These charts were called horoscopes.

Another Greek, the astronomer Ptolemy, added the information from the charts to his maps of the sky. As an astronomer, Ptolemy studied the movements of the stars and planets. But he became an astrologer when he believed without proof that stars and planets affected the lives of human beings.

For the next 2,000 years astrologers and astrology were very popular. Besides all the old beliefs there were some new ones. People began to think that parts of the human body were tied to houses of the zodiac. Astrologers were looked upon as doctors. They treated diseases based on what they saw in the signs and charts of the people who came to see them.

In the 1540s, a Polish-German astronomer, Copernicus, startled everyone with new ideas about what went on in the heavens. He wrote that the Earth did not stand still at the center of a moving universe. He said the

Chaldeans and Ptolemy were wrong. Moreover, there was no such thing as an invisible band or zodiac around the Earth. Instead, he argued that the Earth moved through space circling the sun! Copernicus opened the door to the exact science of astronomy. Gradually, people began to question the unproven ideas of astrologers. They became more interested in astronomers who worked with proven facts.

Today, some people still believe that what takes place in the sky touches our lives on Earth. They need astrologers to tell them how the movements of the stars and planets will make them behave. Astronomers may not agree with this ancient idea. People who need proof before they believe anything may not agree either. Yet, it doesn't hurt for people to know what sign they were born under.

ARIES

MARCH 21–APRIL 19

MARS   **THE HEAD**

MYTH   Phrixus and his sister Helle were to be killed as a gift to the gods by the king and queen of Thessaly. Zeus, king of the Greek gods, sent a golden ram to save them. While they were fleeing on the ram, Helle fell off and drowned. Phrixus made it to safety, but Zeus ordered him to kill the ram. Phrixus slew it and Zeus placed its spirit in the night sky, lighting it forever with bright stars.

TRAITS   Rams are often described as stubborn and daring. Farmers have said that they like to fight, too. Ancient astrologers believed that people born under the sign of Aries were like rams. Since rams fought so much, astrologers claimed that Aries was ruled by Mars, the planet named for the Roman god of war.

CONSTELLATION

TAURUS

APRIL 20–MAY 20

VENUS   **THE NECK**

MYTH   Beautiful Europa, a king's daughter, stood at the water's edge of her tiny land. A bull came by, kneeled before her, and she climbed upon its back. The bull, carrying Europa, loped into the sea and swam to the island of Crete. There the bull changed into his true self—Zeus—and married Europa. To celebrate their wedding, Zeus placed the bull among the stars.

TRAITS   Bulls are steady, strong, stubborn animals that do not anger quickly. People born under the sign of Taurus are thought to be like bulls—steady, strong, stubborn and slow to anger. But if they do become angry, they usually get furious. Astrologers believe they admire art and beauty because Venus, the Roman goddess of beauty and love, rules Taurus.

CONSTELLATION

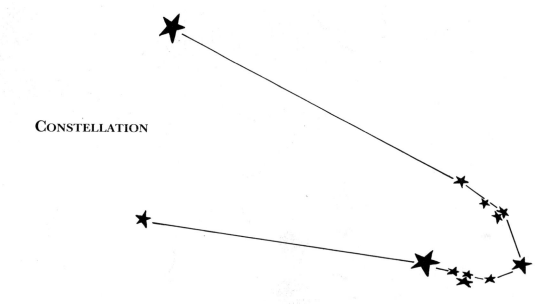

BULL

GEMINI

MAY 21–JUNE 20

MERCURY   **THE ARMS**

MYTH Castor and Pollux were twins and were called the "sons of Zeus." They liked to do everything together and were famous for being good athletes. When Castor was killed in a fight, Pollux asked Zeus to let him die, too. He wanted to be with his brother forever. Zeus granted his wish, and set the twins glowing in the night sky to honor their love for one another.

TRAITS People born under this sign are said to enjoy doing two jobs at once. They are also supposed to change their minds a lot. Mercury, the planet named for the Roman god who carried messages for the gods, rules Gemini. Like Mercury, Gemini people are known to be quick, athletic, and always in touch with others.

CONSTELLATION

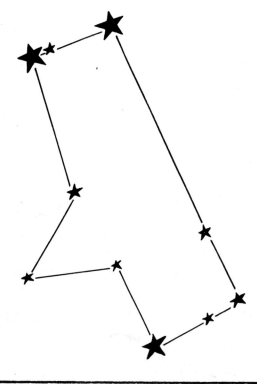

CANCER

JUNE 21–JULY 22

THE MOON   THE CHEST

MYTH   Herakles—or Hercules—half man, half god, was the strongest hero in the ancient world. To test his strength, the gods made him perform twelve labors. After killing a mighty lion, Herakles had to battle Hydra, a monster with nine heads. Hydra was the pet of Hera, queen of the gods. To help the monster, Hera ordered a huge crab, Cancer, to hold Herakles in its great claw while Hydra slew him. But Cancer was no match for the furious Herakles. Herakles crushed the crab and then destroyed Hydra. Zeus, angry with Hera for using the crab to help the monster, placed Cancer among the stars.

TRAITS   The moon rules Cancer. And just as the moon causes changes in the tides, so people born under Cancer are supposed to like change. They are also known to like staying home, the way a crab never leaves its shell. Because a crab is soft on the inside, Cancer people are said to be emotional.

CONSTELLATION

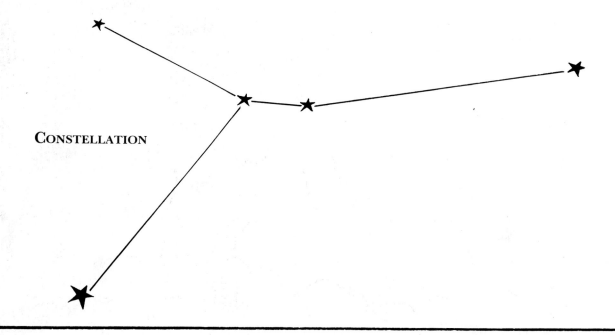

LEO

JULY 23–AUGUST 22

THE SUN

THE HEART

MYTH Nemea, a place in ancient Greece, was famous for its musicians and athletes. Every Nemean lived in fear of a great lion that roamed among them. When Herakles was forced to do twelve labors, the slaying of the Nemean lion headed the list. Herakles strangled the lion with his bare hands. Zeus, Herakles' father, was pleased with his son's success. He added a few more stars to the sky to remember Herakles' victory.

TRAITS Leo is a Latin or Roman word for lion. Leo the Lion is the king of the beasts. Those born under the sign of Leo are said to be like kings. Also, they like to be the center of attention. Since Leo is ruled by the sun, Leo people are usually pleasant, bright, and loving.

CONSTELLATION

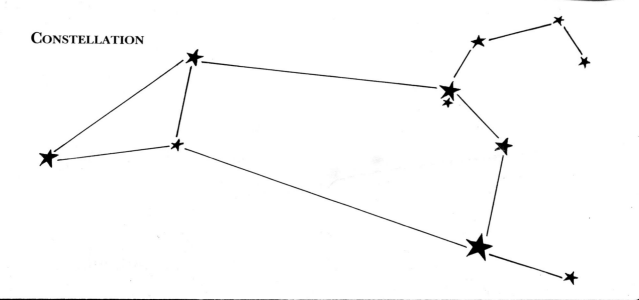

VIRGO

AUGUST 23–SEPTEMBER 22

MERCURY   **THE ABDOMEN**

MYTH   Persephone was the daughter of Demeter, the Greek goddess of the harvest. Persephone was kidnapped by Hades, god of the Lower World. Demeter was so sad that she allowed plants everywhere to die. She asked her brother Zeus for help. Zeus sent Hermes, his messenger, to Hades, seeking Persephone's return. But Persephone had eaten magic fruit that kept her from going back. Later, Zeus and Hades made a bargain. Persephone could spend spring and summer with her mother and fall and winter with Hades. To celebrate Persephone's springtime return, Demeter let the plants grow again. And Zeus created a new set of stars for the sky, called Virgo.

TRAITS   People born under the sign of Virgo are said to be youthful and fussy. They are supposed to enjoy art and beautiful things, too. Because Persephone led two different lives, Virgo people often can do more than one thing well. Mercury, the Roman name for Hermes, rules Virgo. Like Mercury, Virgos enjoy traveling.

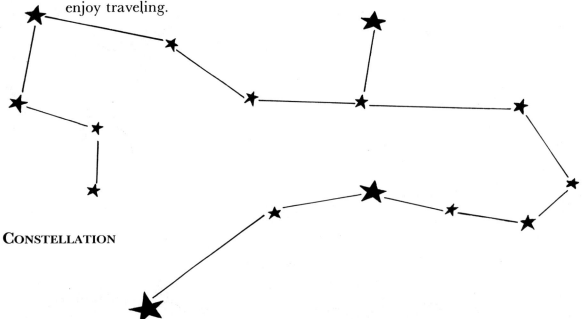

CONSTELLATION

LIBRA

SEPTEMBER 23–OCTOBER 22

VENUS   LOWER BACK

MYTH Aphrodite was the Greek goddess of love. The ancient Romans called her Venus. She adored Adonis, a handsome youth. Her sister Persephone loved him, too. They agreed to share Adonis by having him spend six months with each of them. But soon the sisters quarreled over him. Zeus stepped between them. He ordered Adonis to spend four months with Aphrodite, four months with Persephone, and four months with whomever he pleased. Adonis chose Aphrodite. And in memory of his judgment, Zeus formed the star group Libra—a pair of balanced scales.

TRAITS Librans are peacemakers. They do not like arguments. Librans are ruled by Venus, the Roman Aphrodite. They love beauty and are interested in others. Like Adonis, they often share their feelings with more than one person. Sometimes Librans cannot make decisions. And they are not supposed to be good at keeping secrets, either.

CONSTELLATION

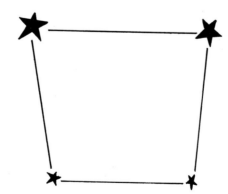

SCALES

SCORPIO

OCTOBER 23–NOVEMBER 21

MARS   **LOWER ABDOMEN**

MYTH   Orion, son of the sea god Poseidon, sometimes killed animals to show off. His friend Artemis, goddess of the hunt, was annoyed by Orion's behavior. One story tells how Artemis dared him to slay a giant scorpion after he had boasted that he could kill all poisonous creatures. When he did, the goddess set the scorpion among the stars. Later, she accidentally killed Orion with an arrow and set him among the stars, too. Another story tells how Artemis, angry over Orion's hunting spree, sent a scorpion to slay him. When it did, Artemis set both Orion and the scorpion among the stars. She wanted to warn hunters not to destroy wildlife without good reason.

TRAITS   Scorpio is ruled by Mars, the planet named for the Roman god of war. Most Scorpios are said to have some of Mars's traits. They are excitable, head-strong, and emotional. Since scorpions are also poisonous, ancient astrologers believed that Scorpios could be dangerous as well as clever and mysterious.

CONSTELLATION

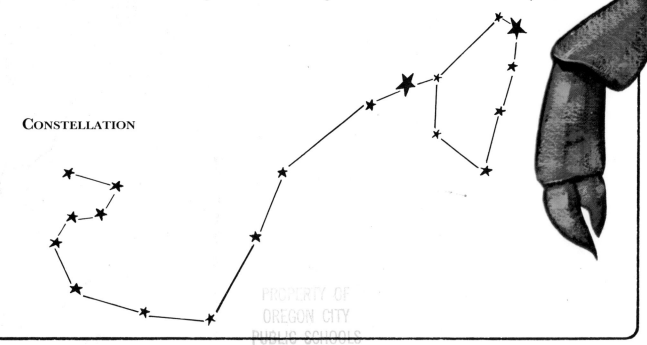

SCORPION

SAGITTARIUS

NOVEMBER 22–DECEMBER 21

JUPITER   **THE HIPS**

MYTH   Chiron was a centaur, a creature that was half man, half horse. Most centaurs were rude and often violent. But Chiron was gentle, fun-loving, and wise. He was taught by the gods. In time, he taught many Greeks who became famous doctors, musicians, hunters, prophets, and archers. Hades, god of the Lower World, tricked Zeus into slaying the centaur with a lightning bolt. Unable to bring Chiron back to life, Zeus gave him a place among the stars as Sagittarius the Archer.

TRAITS   Like Chiron, Sagittarians are said to be gentle, fun-loving, and wise. Since Chiron was an expert archer, Sagittarians are said to be athletic, too. Sagittarius is ruled by Jupiter, the Roman name for Zeus, who is supposed to protect all those born under the sign of the Archer.

CONSTELLATION

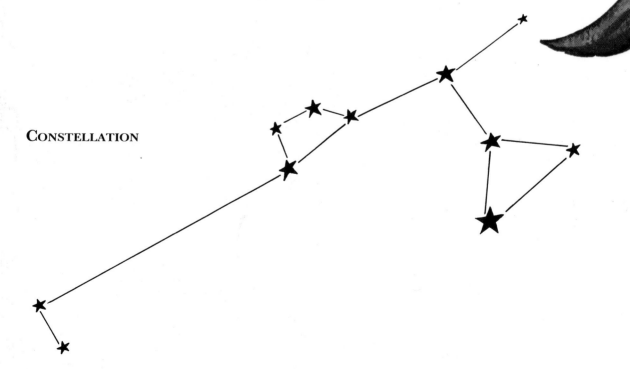

ARCHER

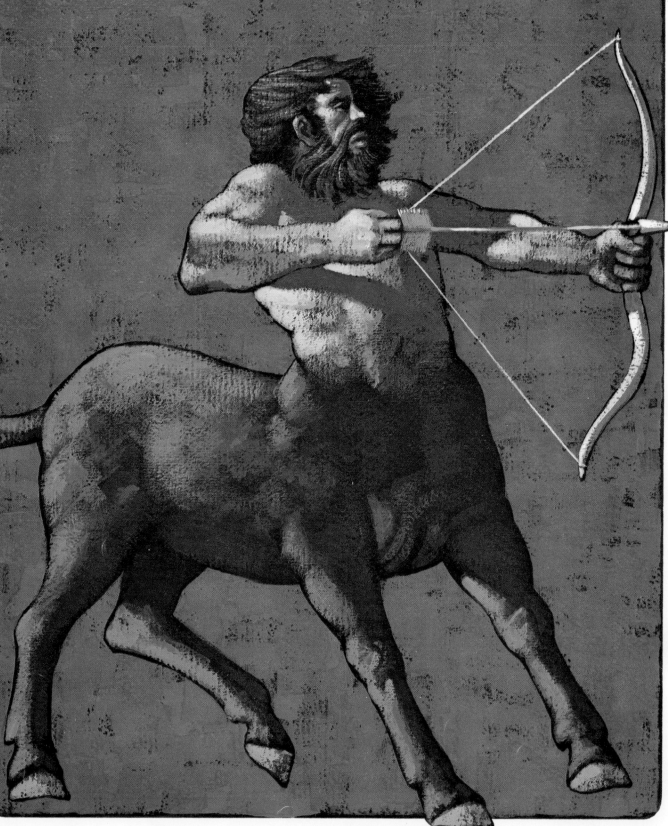

CAPRICORN

DECEMBER 22–JANUARY 19

SATURN   **THE KNEES**

MYTH Capricorn has always been something of a mystery goat. Some ancient astrologers linked Capricorn to Pan. Pan was a mischievous, musical, woodland god—half man, half goat. He liked to frighten young girls and travelers. Others saw Capricorn either as all goat or half goat and half fish. Whatever Capricorn was supposed to be, Zeus placed a goat-fish creature among the stars. He did this to honor a goat-like being whose milk he drank as a baby.

TRAITS Capricorns are said to be as careful and as surefooted as goats. Since goats climb mountains without losing their balance, Capricorns are thought of as steady and ambitious people. Also, Saturn rules Capricorn. And like Saturn, the Greek god Kronos who once ruled the universe, Capricorns make good leaders.

CONSTELLATION

GOAT

AQUARIUS

JANUARY 20–FEBRUARY 18

URANUS

THE ANKLES

MYTH The gods needed a new cupbearer to bring them ambrosia, the liquid that gave them eternal life. Hebe, Hera's daughter and the goddess of youth, no longer wanted to be cupbearer to the gods. Zeus chose Ganymede, the young son of the king of Troy. Disguising himself as an eagle, Zeus swooped down on Ganymede and carried him off to his heavenly home. There he became known among the stars as Aquarius the Water Bearer.

TRAITS Since water is as necessary to human life as ambrosia was to the gods, the Water Bearer became a sign of life. And since the Water Bearer served the gods, Aquarians are known to be giving people. They care about others, yet sometimes like to be by themselves. Also, Aquarians enjoy learning and appreciate art. Uranus, which rules Aquarius, is different from other planets. It has a very sharp tilt. Because of this strangeness, Aquarians are expected to be unusual and creative people.

CONSTELLATION

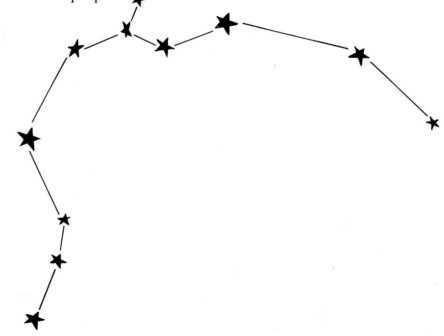

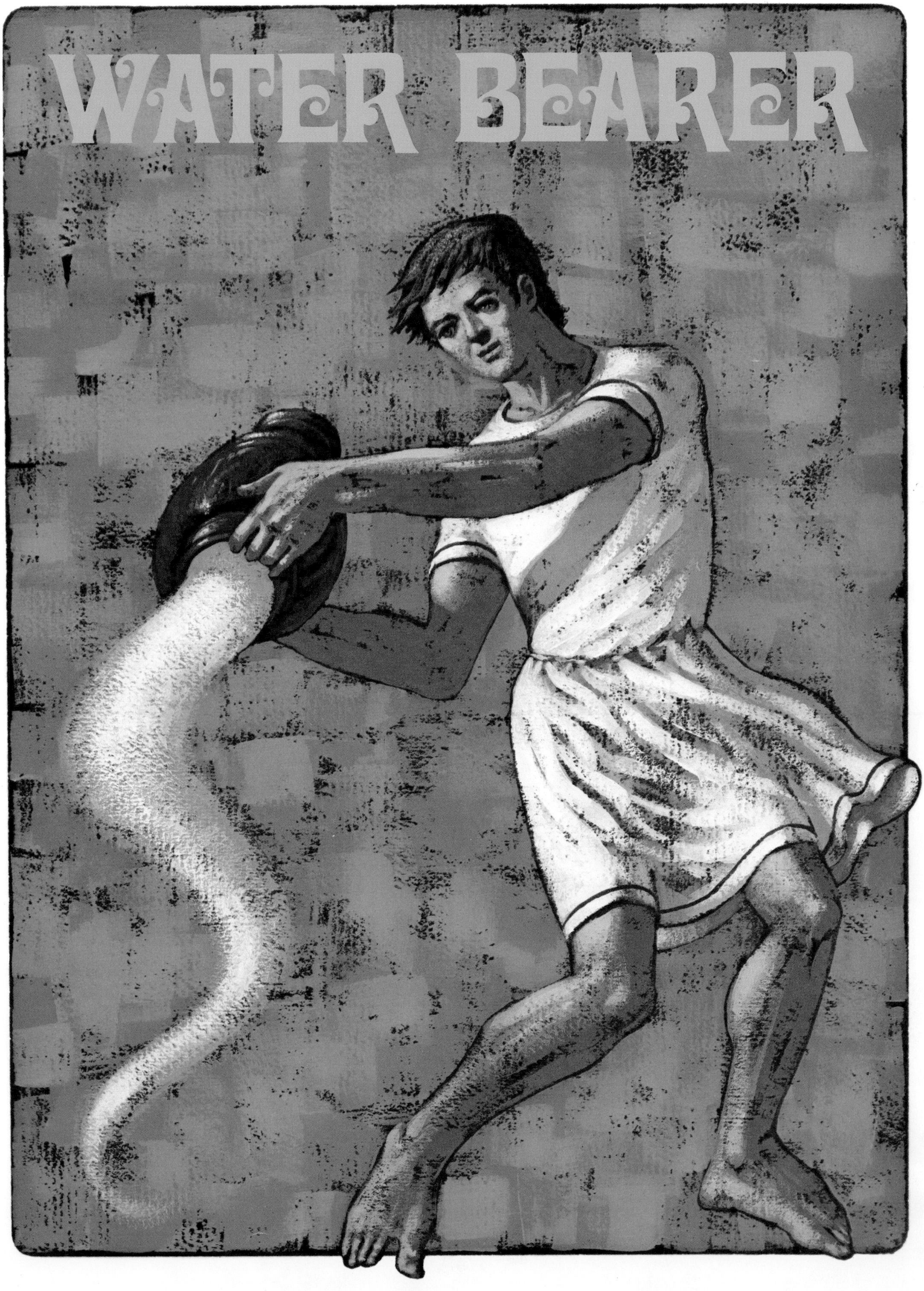
WATER BEARER

PISCES

FEBRUARY 19–MARCH 20

NEPTUNE

THE FEET

MYTH Typhon was the largest, most ferocious monster on Earth. His great head looked like a donkey's, and he spit red hot rocks. His wings were so huge they blocked out the sun. The rest of him—hundreds of great serpents—slithered in every direction at once. Typhon spent most of his time fighting Zeus and the other gods. He even attacked Aphrodite and her son Eros, driving them into the sea. Poseidon, the god of the sea, sent two big fish to rescue them. As Typhon crawled back to his cave, Zeus formed a new group of stars to honor the fish that had saved Aphrodite and Eros. Later, he destroyed Typhon with thunderbolts.

TRAITS Neptune is the Roman name for Poseidon. And like Neptune, who rules Pisces, Pisceans are supposed to swim well. They are not always very brave, preferring to "swim" with the current rather than against it. Like fish that easily swallow worms at the end of a line, Pisceans believe most everything anyone tells them. They keep to themselves and hardly appear in the open, like fish that swim in the dark shadows of the sea.

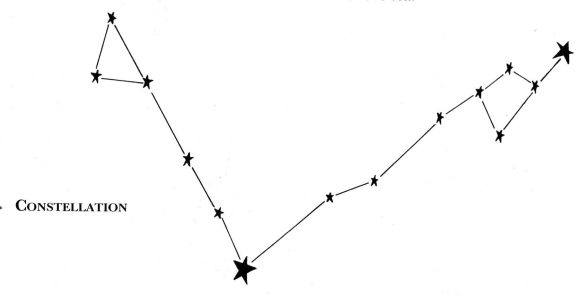

CONSTELLATION

FISH

Each sign of the zodiac has a special symbol:

Aries the Ram

Libra the Scales

Taurus the Bull

Scorpio
the Scorpion

Gemini
the Twins

Sagittarius the Archer

Cancer
the Crab

Capricorn the Goat

Leo the Lion

Aquarius
the Water Bearer

Virgo
the Maiden

Pisces the Fish